BE A MAKER!

MAKER PROJECTS FOR KIDS WHO LOVE

FASHION

SARAH LEVETE

CRABTREE
Publishing Company
www.crabtreebooks.com

Crabtree Publishing Company

www.crabtreebooks.com

Author: Sarah Levete

Publishing plan research and development:
Reagan Miller

Editors: Sarah Eason, Harriet McGregor, Reagan Miller

Proofreaders: Nancy Dickmann, Petrice Custance

Editorial director: Kathy Middleton

Design: Paul Myerscough

Cover design: Emma DeBanks

Photo research: Rachel Blount

**Production coordinator and
  Prepress technician:** Tammy McGarr

Print coordinator: Margaret Amy Salter

Consultant: Chris Stone

Production coordinated by Calcium Creative

Photo Credits:

t=Top, bl=Bottom Left, br=Bottom Right

Danit Peleg: p. 23; Platinum Dirt: p. 25; ReKixx: p. 24; Shutterstock: Africa Studio: p. 22; Samuel Borges Photography: p. 9; Catwalker: p. 4; Diego Cervo: p. 14; Miriam Doerr: p. 5; Everett Collection: p. 19; FashionStock.com: p. 16; Marius Godoi: pp. 1, 26; Sergey Goruppa: p. 8; Jaguar PS: p. 18; Nejron Photo: p. 7; Vanessa Nel: p. 6; Odua Images: p. 11; Sarij: p. 10b; Szefei: p. 10t; Vevchic: p. 15; Techcyled: p. 27; Tudor Photography: pp. 12–13, 20–21, 28–29; Wikimedia Commons: Renaissancechambara: p. 17.

Cover: Tudor Photography.

Library and Archives Canada Cataloguing in Publication

Levete, Sarah, author
       Maker projects for kids who love fashion / Sarah Levete.

(Be a maker!)
Includes index.
Issued in print and electronic formats.
ISBN 978-0-7787-2246-5 (bound).--
ISBN 978-0-7787-2258-8 (paperback).--
ISBN 978-1-4271-1717-5 (html)

       1. Fashion--Juvenile literature. 2. Fashion design--Juvenile literature. I. Title.

TT515.L48 2016   j746.9'2   C2015-907911-X
                                              C2015-907912-8

Library of Congress Cataloging-in-Publication Data

Names: Levete, Sarah, author.
Title: Maker projects for kids who love fashion / Sarah Levete.
Description: Crabtree Publishing Company, [2016] | Series: Be a maker! | Includes index | Description based on print version record and CIP data provided by publisher; resource not viewed.
Identifiers: LCCN 2015045214 (print) | LCCN 2015044049 (ebook) | ISBN 9781427117175 (electronic HTML) | ISBN 9780778722465 (reinforced library binding : alk. paper) | ISBN 9780778722588 (pbk. : alk. paper)
Subjects: LCSH: Fashion--Juvenile literature. | Fashion design--Juvenile literature.
Classification: LCC TT507 (print) | LCC TT507 .L4475 2016 (ebook) | DDC 746.9/2--dc23
LC record available at http://lccn.loc.gov/2015045214

Crabtree Publishing Company

www.crabtreebooks.com   1-800-387-7650

Printed in Canada/022016/MA20151130

Published in Canada
Crabtree Publishing
616 Welland Ave.
St. Catharines, Ontario
L2M 5V6

Published in the United States
Crabtree Publishing
PMB 59051
350 Fifth Avenue, 59th Floor
New York, New York 10118

Published in the United Kingdom
Crabtree Publishing
Maritime House
Basin Road North, Hove
BN41 1WR

Published in Australia
Crabtree Publishing
3 Charles Street
Coburg North
VIC, 3058

CONTENTS

TIME TO MAKE!

From the way a room is decorated to the style of a jacket, fashion is all around. French fashion designer Coco Chanel once said, "Fashion is not something that exists in dresses only. Fashion is in the sky, in the street, fashion has to do with ideas, the way we live, what is happening." In this book, we explore the fashion of clothes and **accessories**, what inspires their designers, how fashion is an expression of identity, and how you can become a maker to create your own style.

BEING A MAKER

The maker philosophy is about trying new things and creating new possibilities. Makers persist and do not give up at the first hurdle. In fashion, makers draw on both creative and practical skills, such as an understanding of color or the ability to cut out a delicate stencil design. Makers often collaborate, or work together, in **makerspaces** and labs. They gather to share supplies, tools, and knowledge.

Fashion can be fun, funky, and **functional**. Does this design inspire you or make you want to change it to suit your style?

Share your ideas with your friends—see what you can come up with together. Fashion is for anyone and everyone. Boys, girls, men, and women of all ages can become fashion makers. And remember, fashion is more than clothes. From bags and hats to key chains and jewelry, accessories can transform a plain outfit into one that is both personalized and stylish. Making is cheap, fun, and endlessly inventive.

WHERE TO START

You do not need a sewing machine for any of the projects in this book, nor do you need to be good at sewing. All you need are some ideas and a willingness to make a start. All of the projects invite you to add your own twist—be adventurous and see where your fashion journey will take you. You can use the techniques in this book to **modify** and enhance your own clothes, but remember to check with your parent or guardian before making any fashion changes to your clothes. You may become inspired to make your own clothes from scratch, so why not check out the Internet for more making techniques? Creating a new look or piece of clothing does not always go as planned, but makers see challenges as opportunities to develop ideas and learn.

Use any materials you have on hand, or even knit your own!

THE STORY OF FASHION

We wear clothes to keep warm and to cover parts of our bodies. However, if that was the only purpose of clothes, everyone would wear the same materials in identical ways. Instead, clothing choices are very personal, and match our mood, situation, and personality. Fashion is also influenced by the time period in which we live, by geography, and by society. Think about what fashion means to you.

FUNCTION OR FASHION?

Some clothes are purely functional. A spacesuit is not designed to look good. It is designed to allow astronauts to perform their jobs safely and effectively. Some clothes are both functional and fashionable. For example, pockets on a jacket or on pants serve a purpose. However, they will have been styled in some way by the designer to give a certain look.

This girl's hat, boots, and leggings keep her warm, but they have also been fashioned to look stylish.

WEARING MONEY

Fashion and clothing have long been linked to wealth and **status** in the world. In the past, wealthier people could afford more luxurious materials that were often highly decorated. Those with less money and a lower status wore simpler clothes made from basic fabrics. Ancient Romans wore long robes called togas that draped around the body. A Roman man wearing a toga showed that he was an important citizen of Rome. Roman women wore long, pleated garments called stola. Roman children from wealthy families wore a **tunic** with a purple border. Purple dye was very expensive, so wearing any purple in Roman times demonstrated the family's wealth.

Today, there is no formal link between fashion and status, although many expensive materials and designer clothes clearly show the wearer's financial status.

Wearing certain clothes tells people something about the wearer's role and status in society.

Be a Maker!

Fashion tells a story. Take a look at the clothes you and your friends wear. Think about what you wear to school and in your free time. Think about the factors that influence your choice of clothes or the way that they have been designed. Do you follow trends **and dress like your** peers**? Do you change what you wear according to your mood? Perhaps you could add accessories to personalize your look?**

CHANGING FASHION

Fashion is constantly changing. What we wear, how we wear it, and why we wear it tell us a lot about the society and time we live in. Innovators and their inventions have transformed our ability to make clothes, and have influenced the materials used. Changes in society have allowed people to adopt new types of clothing—some of which we take for granted today!

INVENTIONS

During the period known as the Industrial Revolution in the 1700s, the makers of the time designed new machinery that could spin thread and make new types of fabrics. In 1764, James Hargreaves invented the spinning jenny. This machine had multiple spools onto which thread was spun for weaving into cloth. It then became quicker and cheaper to produce clothes.

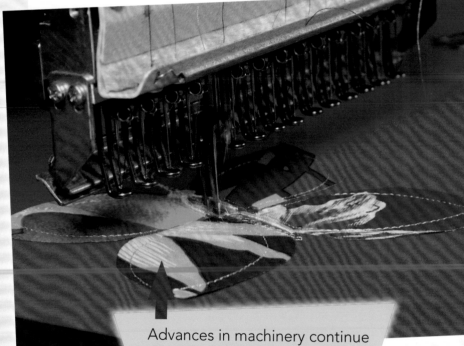

Advances in machinery continue to make it easier and cheaper to create fashion items.

Be a Maker!

Choose a period of history. Look at the fashion worn by both the wealthy and less wealthy. What do their clothes tell you about their lives and the period in which they lived? See if you can make links with social and technological features of the period.

SEWING MACHINES

In the 1800s, the invention of the sewing machine meant sewing no longer relied on **laborious** hand stitching. In France, England, Germany, and the United States, several inventors worked on creating versions of the sewing machine. These inventors were early makers. James Gibbs—one of the men who played a part in the inventions— said, "No useful sewing machine was ever invented by one man; and all first attempts to do work by machinery, previously done by hand, have been failures. It is only after several able inventors have failed in attempt, that someone with the mental powers to combine the efforts of others with his own, at last produces a practicable sewing machine."

SOCIETY'S INFLUENCE

Today, in most **cultures**, both boys and girls wear pants, but it was not always so! Until the 1920s, in Western countries, it was unacceptable for women and girls to wear pants. In Eastern countries, however, women and men were free to wear them. During the 1920s and 1930s, more and more women began wearing pants in North America, but amazingly women were not allowed to wear them on the United States Senate floor until 1993!

In some parts of the world, up until the 1900s, it was frowned upon for women to wear pants. Today, it is common.

AROUND THE WORLD

Inspiration for fashion comes from across the world. Many countries and cultures have **traditional** clothes. For example, in Japan, kimonos are often worn for special occasions and ceremonies. In some cultures, fashion is less important than practical considerations, such as wearing clothes suited for climate or work.

STITCH-FREE

Not all clothes are sewn together. For hundreds of years, women in Asian countries such as India, Sri Lanka, and Bangladesh have worn saris. A sari is a long strip of unstitched cloth from 13–30 feet (4–9 m) long. It is usually wrapped around the waist, with one end draped over the shoulder. Brightly colored saris are often highly decorated with elaborate embroidery or precious stones. An item called a tobe, which is a long piece of fabric wrapped around the body, is worn in some rural parts of Sudan.

FASHIONING THE WORLD

The Maasai people in eastern Kenya wear distinctive traditional garments, such as the shuka, and highly beaded jewelry. The shuka is a cloth, often a **vibrant** red, worn around the body. Maasai women meet regularly to work together on the complex beading used in bangles and necklaces that the Maasai wear.

Saris can be worn as everyday clothing, or can be worn for elaborate and special occasions. Maasai bangles have bright colors and beautiful designs.

Some well-known designers take inspiration from Maasai designs, and some are working in partnership with the Maasai community, drawing on their unique skills and knowledge. For example, the successful Australian design company "Sass and Bide" has joined up with a group of Maasai craftswomen to use their handiwork and skills on the company's designs. The women receive a fair wage, which helps pay toward their children's education, and gives them **financial independence**.

FASHIONING RELIGION

Many Muslims believe that women should not show their legs in public, so in many Muslim countries, women's fashion is based around long pants, dresses, or leggings. Often, Muslim women wear long scarves called hijabs to cover their hair. Experimenting with patterns and colors can turn a plain scarf into a fashionable item.

Patterned fabric or bright colors transform a traditional hijab.

Be a Maker!

What influences a country's fashion? Think about the environment, the landscape, and the climate. How do beliefs influence what people in your community choose to wear? Select a culture or geographical area different from yours to research. Can you conclude anything about that culture or area based on the fashions worn?

MAKE IT!
GET SEWING

You can glue, tape, or even staple materials together, but the most common way is to sew. Putting pieces of material together is a key step in fashion designing. This project teaches you how to do a running stitch, which is one of the most widely used techniques for holding two pieces of fabric together. As you practice, expect to make errors. With a little **persistence** you can learn from your mistakes and adjust your approach as necessary. You can join fabrics to make a fashion item such as a purse, belt, headband, or wristband.

YOU WILL NEED
- Two or more pieces of fabric
- Sharp scissors
- Needle and thread (a piece of thread about the length of your arm, threaded through the eye of the needle, with a knot tied on the loose end)

1

- Choose two pieces of fabric. You may have fabric from clothes that you have outgrown, but make sure to check with a parent or guardian before you use them! Or why not visit a thrift store and look for fabrics with interesting **textures**, colors, or patterns?
- Cut your material to the shapes you need. For your first try, it will be easier to join together two straight edges.

2

- Place the two pieces of fabric together, with the sides you want displayed on the finished item facing in. Be sure that the edges you want to sew together are perfectly lined up.
- At the beginning of one edge, push the needle through the fabric and pull gently until you reach the knot at the end of the thread.
- Push the needle back through the fabric (the same side your needle has pushed through) about 0.2 inches (5 mm) from the spot where you first pushed the needle through the fabric.
- Pull the needle through to make your first stitch.
- Repeat, pushing the needle through the fabric, leaving about 0.2 inches (5 mm) between each stitch.
- Continue along the length of the fabric.

3

- When you reach the end of the edge, cut the needle from the thread and tie off the thread with a knot to prevent the stitches from unraveling.
- Now think about how you can use this newly created material.

CONCLUSION

Look at the stitching. Are the stitches even or are some long and some short? Gently tug the seam of your material. Does it pull apart or have you sewn it together strongly enough?

Make It Even Better!

What alternative ways can be used to join the pieces of fabric, and what are the benefits or disadvantages of these methods? What can you do with this material? Think about other ways to use it. Can you turn it into a bag as a gift for a friend? If you want the material to have an opening that can be closed and opened, how can this be achieved?

FASHION DESIGN

Today, you can buy inexpensive fashion items from many popular stores. These clothes are mass-produced (made in large numbers). More expensive clothes are those with a designer **label**. Extremely expensive clothes are called **haute couture**. Creating your own designs means you are in control of your style instead of a company—and it is much cheaper!

THE PROCESS

The making process for a line of clothing can take about 18 months from design to store. Designers research what they think will be popular. They check out other fashion shows and try to predict trends for the upcoming season. They then create a **mood board** to reflect the themes or ideas for their new designs. A mood board is a collage of images, pieces of material, colors, and textures. The mood board visually expresses the style the designer is aiming for. Then the designer researches different **textiles** and narrows down the color choices. Creating sketches helps the designer to visualize their ideas. Some designers use Computer-Aided Design (CAD) to do this on screen. Designers need technical drawing skills to make the detailed **patterns** from which their clothes will be made.

Once a designer has gathered ideas on a mood board, he or she will work from sketches of their designs.

MUSIC

Music can have a huge influence on fashion. In the 1960s, a group called The Beatles took the world by storm—and so did their style and fashion sense. When their manager bought some tight-fitting boots with slight heels and pointed toes, they proved so popular with people around the world that they became known as Beatles Boots! Today, the fashion for baggy clothes and gold chains reflects the influence of hip-hop music.

PUNK STYLE

Punk rock is a music style that began in the mid 1970s in the United States and in the United Kingdom. Punk fashion and style developed alongside the music scene. The punk look was about individuals dressing however they wanted. People decorated their clothes with safety pins and chains, and wore ripped pants and spiked hairstyles called mohawks.

The punk look featured deliberate rips and tears in clothes.

Be a Maker!

Creating a mood board helps makers visually express ideas. Do you have ideas for designing clothes or accessories? Make a mood board to help develop your ideas. Your mood board might include pieces of colorful fabric that inspire you or sketches of design ideas.

HIGH FASHION

The extravagant designs that hit the catwalks during international fashion shows often influence new clothing trends.

WHAT IS HAUTE COUTURE?

Haute couture literally translates from the French as "high sewing," although the term has come to mean exclusive high-end fashion. Haute couture clothing is extravagant, handcrafted, and hand-fitted, and it costs a lot of money. The designs are made from the most luxurious, expensive, high-quality materials. They often feature incredible detail, such as sequins, sparkling jewels, and even real flowers.

Fashion shows feature new designs that are often then copied and sold more cheaply in stores.

HAUTE COUTURE MAKERS

People rather than machinery play an important role in haute couture. Everything is sewn by hand. It can take more than 200 hours to create one item of clothing. In France, a trade organization called the "*Chambre de commerce et d'industrie de Paris*" sets strict rules about which designers qualify as haute couture. Each **fashion house** must have a workshop for designing clothes in Paris, employ more than 20 staff, and must be able to present two fashion shows a year. These shows feature the most extraordinary clothes.

PRACTICAL FASHION?

Designer Hussein Chalayan is an inspired maker. At one of his fashion shows, a table was set up in front of the audience. A model stepped into the middle of the table, which transformed into a wooden skirt! Hussein, who was born in Cyprus, says, "I'm interested in the impossible, generally speaking. I think that informs almost every aspect of my life . . . I am an artist and a designer, if you want to categorize me, but ultimately I'm interested in ideas."

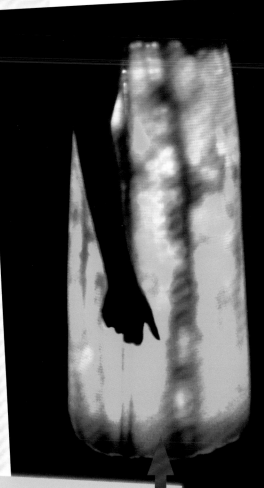

Hussein Chalayan features light emitting diodes (LEDs) on this dress.

Makers and Shakers

Charles Frederick Worth

Charles Worth (1825–1895) viewed clothing as an art form and is often considered the father of haute couture. He worked as an **apprentice** to two textile merchants. During this time, he visited art galleries to study historical portraits and grow his design ideas. He set up his own successful business and introduced changes we still see today—he had his label sewn into the back of clothes and used real models, rather than mannequins, to show off his clothes to clients.

Fashion is not just about the design of clothes. It is also about people who help set trends. Stars, **stylists**, and designers want to inspire the latest fashion trends.

SHOCKERS!

Some stars like to use clothes to shock or make a statement. In the 1930s, singer and dancer Josephine Baker wore a skirt made from 16 bananas in a performance called *La Folie du Jour*. This show propelled her to international fame. Josephine Baker's fashion sense had a lasting impact. In 2006, singer Beyoncé performed a tribute to Josephine wearing a banana skirt.

At the MTV Awards in 2010, American performer and singer Lady Gaga wore a dress made from pieces of raw beef. Lady Gaga's stylist, Nicola Formichetti, asked Argentinian designer Franc Ferdinand to help her create a dress made from meat. Before the awards, Ferdinand sewed through the slabs of meat draped around Lady Gaga. The dress made headlines, but it did not kick-start a trend for meat garments!

Lady Gaga's raw meat dress and headwear caused a sensation when she appeared at the MTV Awards.

GETTING SEEN

Most designers show off their high-end fashion by lending celebrities their exclusive clothes to wear at high-profile public events where there are sure to be photographers! When model turned designer Kate Moss was seen in a dress she had designed for a popular store, it sold out in 15 minutes!

Naomi Watts wears a Stella McCartney dress, providing the designer with great free publicity.

Makers and Shakers

Tavi Gevinson

Recently, fashion bloggers have played a role in setting trends. American Tavi Gevinson (born 1996) started her fashion blogging career at age 11. She loved style and design magazines. Her interest soon led to action. She set up a **blog** called *Style Rookie*. The blog featured pictures of the young Tavi in which she had created unique fashion looks. *Style Rookie* attracted thousands of viewers. At age 15, Tavi set up an online magazine, *Rookie*, featuring fashion ideas and articles. "*Rookie* isn't about having the answers—it's a place where we can discuss issues and work them out."

19

MAKE IT!
BRAIDING

Take a simple cotton T-shirt and use braiding to transform it into a fashion item with a new neckline. These **upcycled** T-shirts also make excellent and surprising gifts!

1 ● Cut tiny holes around the front of the T-shirt neckline, about one fingertip apart. If you find it difficult to cut the holes, pinch the T-shirt to snip off a tiny section. This creates a hole.

2 ● Tie a knot in one end of a strip of fabric.

3
- Start at one end of the neckline. Place the knot near the first hole on the inside of the T-shirt.
- Push the strip a short way through the first hole to make a loop.
- Push another small loop up through the second hole.
- Holding the loops together, push the second loop underneath and through the first loop.
- Push up a loop through the third hole and then under and through the second loop.

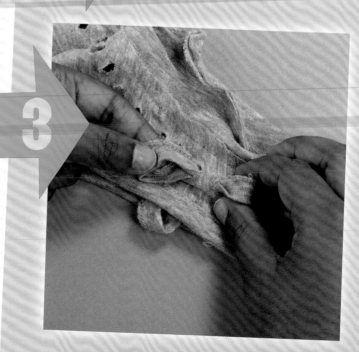

4

- Repeat the looping process, each time creating a new loop and pushing it up and through the previous one.
- Continue until you reach the end of the neckline.
- Make a knot on the inside of the T-shirt when you reach the end. You may want to stitch both knots in place.

CONCLUSION

Try the T-shirt on. How does the braiding look? Why do you think the braiding has shortened the length of the T-shirt? You may want to experiment with holes spaced wider apart or closer together. Or experiment with colors—you could braid with different colored strips of fabric.

Make It Even Better!

Experiment with braiding sleeves—it uses the same principle but goes all the way around the hand end of the sleeve. Think about how you could braid a T-shirt by cutting slits down the length of the T-shirt. Try it! Experiment by using wide or narrow fabric strips.

MATERIAL WORLD

Fashion needs fabric. From colors to textures, fabric is the very essence of fashion. Makers experiment with materials that have different properties, which determines the function of a fashion item and its cost. Thick wool is not useful for fashionable sportswear and silk is not be practical for everyday clothes. Fashion and science meet as makers research ways to create new textiles.

DENIM

This fabric is ideal for makers who need to create clothes that are durable. Denim jeans were first designed for men working on the farms and mines in the western United States in the late nineteenth century. A **tailor** named Jacob Davis was asked to make a pair of strong pants for a local woodcutter. Like any good maker, he collaborated with a fabric supplier, Levi Strauss, and denim jeans were created.

NYLON

Nylon is a **synthetic** material made from chemicals. It created a fashion sensation when it first appeared in 1939. Expensive silk stockings that women wore under their dresses to cover their legs were replaced by cheaper nylon ones. In just one day, 72,000 pairs of nylon stockings were sold when they first went on sale in New York City in 1940.

Walk down any street and you will most likely see someone wearing a pair of denim jeans.

DESIGN AND PRINT

Fast developments in **three-dimensional (3-D)** printing technology may soon make it easy to print out wearable clothes. Artist and maker Kade Chan created and printed a pair of 3-D high heels using a 3-D doodle pen!

SMART

Smart fabrics, or e-textiles, combine electronics and fabric to create fabrics that have the ability to do things such as change color, size, and even temperature. They may be responsive to swipes and taps, just like a computer screen. Or perhaps makers will develop athletic clothing that monitors the wearers body temperature and helps cool the wearers down when he or she gets too warm.

Israeli fashion student Danit Peleg printed her design collection from home—using a 3-D printer!

Be a Maker!

Which of these has already been created: a dress made from balloons, from toilet paper, or from a phone book? The answer is all of them! Present a case for using an unusual material in a fashion design. Choose the item you want to make and the material you will use. Will your design choice be environmentally friendly or simply be something new and innovative.

ECO FASHION

Ask your older relatives if they bought a lot of clothes when they were young, or whether they had a few items that they wore over and over. Today, fashions come and go. Mass-produced clothes mean that we buy and get rid of clothes quickly. The Environmental Protection Agency reports that the average American throws away 70 pounds (32 kg) of clothing per year—only 15 percent of used clothing is recycled.

THIRSTY COTTON, PRECIOUS WATER

It takes 713 gallons (2,700 L) of water to make a cotton T-shirt! Pesticides are used to protect cotton crops from damage. Once picked, cotton is treated with chemicals to protect it from moth damage and staining and it is flown around the world for processing and clothing production.

These sneakers are made from materials that are 100 percent recyclable. The entire shoe can be recycled and used to make a new one!

ETHICAL FASHION

Stella McCartney is a very successful designer of **ethical** clothing, shoes, and accessories. A strict vegetarian and an animal rights advocate, she refuses to use leather (from animal skin) or fur in any of her designs. McCartney chooses her materials and sources with extreme care: "I believe in creating pieces that aren't going to get burned, that aren't going to landfills, that aren't going to damage the environment." Even Stella's stores are powered by renewable energy.

Makers and Shakers

Gary Harvey

Makers have respect for their environment, and in fashion an easy way to demonstrate this is to recycle or upcycle clothing. Gary Harvey is an **eco-designer**. He designs dresses made from recycled goods. He has made dresses using newspapers, old army jackets, and bottle caps!

CHANGE IT!

You could turn a T-shirt into a bag or try new techniques to give a twist to old clothes. Recycle by setting up a clothing swap with friends—everyone contributes an item of clothing and takes home a different item of clothing. You can buy from thrift stores and donate unwanted clothes. Ask your family to give you their unwanted clothes so you can design something new from them. Fashion is not just clothes. That old T-shirt can be transformed into a cushion or a hair accessory. Think creatively!

This leather jacket has been made from the leather taken from the seats of an old car!

ACCESSORIZE

Fashion is not just the clothes you wear. It is the things that go with it, from headbands to ankle bracelets. Some accessories such as jewelry are purely decorative while others, such as belts and bags, combine function and fashion. A plain shirt can be transformed by the addition of an accessory and handmade accessories make great gifts!

BUTTONED UP

Nearly any material can be used to create accessories. Get creative, talk with friends about the accessories they like, and notice accessories being worn by people who pass you on the street. Buttons, beads, newspaper, pencils—these can all be turned into fabulous accessories. Buttons keep clothes fastened, but they can also be used to decorate a belt or turned into a pair of earrings. Dress up a pair of plain gloves with brightly colored buttons and beads. Transform old sneakers with patterned laces—experiment with braiding your own laces using strips of fabric made from old clothing. Strips of newspaper can become **papier-mâché** earrings or pins.

Be inventive! Use a pair of jeans you have grown out of and turn them into a funky bag!

26

GLOVED UP

Gloves are accessories that have a function—they keep hands warm and protected from the elements. In the 1500s, wealthy women and men wore gloves made from chicken skin and the skin of unborn calves, because they were believed to keep the skin soft. Both men and women wore scented gloves in the 1600s. A woman would give her partner a glove as a token of her love.

What happens to old computers? Their circuit boards and wires can be turned into stunning jewelry!

Makers and Shakers

Annika Lo

Annika Lo has been a fashion maker since she was a small girl. Her interest began when she was only six years old and looked at a book about fashion technology. Since then, she has combined her interest in fashion with soft circuits. Lo creates designs that often feature lights! At one Maker Faire, her temperature-sensing light-up belt did not perform as expected, but in true maker style, the young designer said: "At Maker Faire when I was showing my creation it was never accurate. This was frustrating! But debugging is a part of making so whatcha gonna do?"

MAKE IT!
STENCILING

Stenciling is a fantastic technique that can be used on different materials. The stencil is a shape of your choosing—it can be text, a pattern, an image, or any design you like. Pair the stencil with a variety of colors, patterns, and fabrics and you can make a stunning creation.

● To make your stencil, draw or print a design onto cardboard and carefully cut out the shape. For your first attempt, keep your design simple.

1

2

● Place some more cardboard on the inside of your item on which you plan to paint to prevent paint leaking through to the other side, and to provide a firmer painting surface.
● Place the stencil over the fabric of your item and position it where you want the stencil to be seen. Tape it in place.

- Paint in the cut-out space of the stencil.
- Remove the stencil. Leave the paint to dry.
- After 24 hours, ask an adult to help you iron the painted portion of the fabric. This helps to set the paint.

3

4

- The image should remain even when the garment is washed—but make sure you do not wash any other clothes with it the first time in case some paint comes off.
- Add any other decorations you like to your fabric using fabric glue or sewing—you could try buttons, badges, or even shells!

CONCLUSION

How does the stenciled image look? Are the colors strong? Could they be made bolder by overlaying different colors? Are the edges of the design sharp? Would changing the fabric type result in sharper edges?

Make It Even Better!

A stencil made from cardboard will not hold up well after being painted a few times. What else can you use to create a stronger stencil shape? Can you decorate using stencils with more intricate designs? Experiment with alternative ways to decorate your item and above all, enjoy your making experience!

GLOSSARY

Please note: Some bold-faced words are defined where they appear in the text

accessories Fashion items such as hats, gloves, bags, and jewelry

apprentice Someone who is learning a trade from an employer

blog An individual's website, frequently updated with their latest news

cultures Ideas and customs of particular people or societies

eco-designer A designer who has a respect for environmental issues

ethical Conforming to a moral code or having an awareness of moral issues

fashion house A company that designs and sells high-fashion garments

financial independence The ability to live without relying on someone else for money

functional Serving a purpose

haute couture Fashion houses or designers that create exclusive and often trend-setting fashions

label A brand name

laborious Describes a task requiring hard and detailed effort

makerspaces Places where makers gather to innovate, share resources, and learn from one another

modify To change

mood board A visual collection (photographs/drawings/pieces of fabric) of ideas and thoughts

nylon A synthetic material that is strong yet flexible, and cheap

papier-mâché A mixture of paper and glue that becomes hard when dry

patterns Drawings from which the parts of a garment are traced onto fabric before being cut out and sewn

peers People of the same age group

persistence The action of continuing and not giving up easily

status Social standing

stylists People whose job it is to make things or other people look good

synthetic Human-made

tailor A person who makes clothes to fit a specific individual

textiles A type of cloth or woven fabric

textures The feel or appearance of surfaces

three-dimensional (3-D) An image that has height, width, and gives the impression of depth

traditional Something that has been established for a long time

trends The latest fashions or styles

tunic A loose fitting item of clothing, often sleeveless, that extends to the knees

upcycled Reinvented by adding or changing in some way

vibrant Lively and bright

LEARNING MORE

BOOKS

Albee, Sarah. *Why'd They Wear That?: Fashion as the Mirror of History.* National Geographic Kids, 2015.

Galen, Marjorie. *The Fashion Designer's Handbook & Fashion Kit: Learn to Sew and Become a Designer in 33 Fabulous Projects.* Workman Publishing, 2012.

Teen Vogue Editors. *The Teen Vogue Handbook: An Insider's Guide to Careers in Fashion.* Razorbill, 2009.

WEBSITES

Check out this website for lots of sewing project ideas, from bags and flags to cushions and toys:
www.freekidscrafts.com/techniques/sewing-projects

Packed with style, this website shares inspiration and skills. Step-by-step instructions and pictures will help you create your own designs at:
www.ispydiy.com

This website provides a lot of useful links to maker fashion projects at:
www.makezine.com

Discover 24 new fashion making ideas at:
www.stylemotivation.com/24-stylish-diy-clothing-tutorials

INDEX